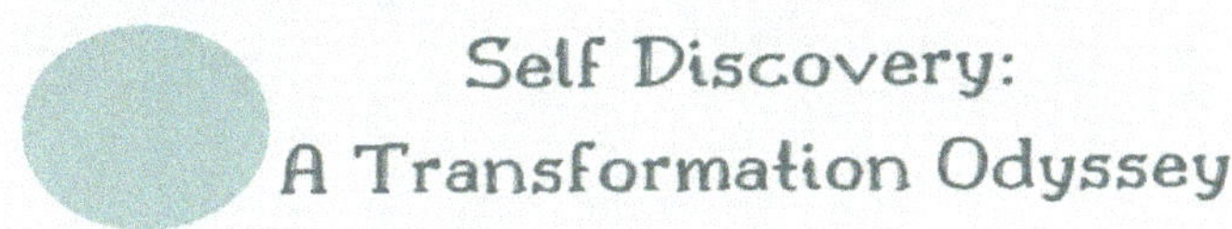

Self Discovery:
A Transformation Odyssey

Self-Discovery: A Transformation Odyssey
Copyright ©2025 by Judith E. Ramos-Pérez
Published 2025
First Edition

The methodologies and experiences shared in this book are merely the author's perspective. It is always recommended to seek support from professional experts in the field.

Cover design by Judith E. Ramos

Library of Congress Cataloging-in-Publication Data has been applied for.

Print ISBN- **979-8-218-99724-3**

Printed in the United States of America

v.20250407

Acknowledgements

To my devoted husband, Edwin, whose unwavering love, and support have guided me through every decision, even those than might be perceived as impossible and crazy ones. You are my rock. 143!!!

To my daughters, Hei, Arbie, and Heiza, your belief in me and unhesitating encouragement to embark on this new journey mean the world. Your reminder that we are Strong Women capable of anything we set our minds to fuels my spirit.

To Melissa, my college friend turned sister, your coaching illuminated the path of self-care.

Your guidance taught me that prioritizing myself is not selfish, but an act of self-love.

To Katia, my cherished "Cara Amica e Sorella," your constant reminders that authenticity, transparency, and vulnerability are acts of courage, not weakness, are my guiding lights. Thank you for standing by me, especially during the darkest times and for being always my "Aliada"!

To my beloved mom and dad, my angels in heaven, Papi Soto, thank you for watching over us. Mami Esther, your sage advice echoes in my heart, urging me to do more and care for myself so I can care for my family. Your presence, even beyond this life, remains my ultimate inspiration. I love and miss you dearly.

To Carl, my colleague and fellow writer, your role as my writing accountability partner has been invaluable. Thank you for introducing me to new tools that have transformed this dream into a tangible reality.

Lastly, but certainly not least, to all my family members and friends who have made this new reality possible: your unwavering support and reminders that where one door closes, another opens, have been my guiding force. Your belief in me has been pivotal. Thank you for reminding me to always BELIEVE!

Contents

Life often hands us lemons, challenging us to make lemonade or moreover craft Limoncello.

Navigating life's unpredictable and wicket twists can be as grueling as running a marathon or enduring a contest. Each day brings new, unexpected challenges, disrupting any notion of routine. Adaptation, change, and self-reinvention become essential in this relentless journey.

Everyone faces a choice: learn from life's challenges (those lemons life throws at us) or let them decay into wasted opportunities. To truly thrive, we must change and adapt, exploring into our innermost selves. It is a daunting task, demanding unstoppable and consistent determination.

This introspective journey is pivotal for success, demanding we confront truths about ourselves. It is akin to gazing into a mirror, acknowledging imperfections that compel us to understand why life presents challenges. Growth mandates leaving behind burdens, even people (including toxic family and friends), to progress toward our goals. It requires the ultimate sacrifice: Being **truthful to ourselves**.

This is not a call to live life in fast-forward, driving "Fast and Furious" nor too slow, yet a plea to find our optimal pace. Self-competition, not against others, but against our former selves, is the true race.

Ask yourself: What is your ultimate aspiration? What impedes your pursuit of excellence (not happiness as happiness is just an emotional state in a specific time span)? Shedding limitations and embracing change is solely your responsibility. To achieve excellence, one must balance equations unique to our respective life's journey.

We are all bestowed with distinct traits that I called superpowers and with that... multiple responsibilities. Comparing ourselves to others, rather than our past selves, hampers growth. Everyone's path to success is different; your superpower dictates the balance needed to evolve into your best self. No one can make the changes you need to be your best self. You only have the power to transform and get out of the cocoon akin a butterfly.

Embracing your unique superpower is the catalyst for transformation. Remember that your own experiences will mold your mind and spirit. Your recipe for life's lemons will not be the same as others. Often people make lemonade, others

Limoncello, margaritas, or even key lime pie. Our

uniqueness dictates the way we excel and evolve

and the pace that supports our transformation.

Can you get the picture?

HOW
TO
START

Unveiling the WHY

Initiating change, regardless of its nature, demands time and introspection. This temporal investment is pivotal to comprehend the necessity for change, the urge to metamorphose into an improved rendition of oneself. No one else will spearhead the changes required as it is a journey that you must undertake solely.

Identifying your WHY becomes the cornerstone, anchoring you throughout this transformational odyssey. It is this rationale that propels the journey, guiding each step with a clear endpoint in mind. The realization of your WHY might not be singular. You start with one, yet along this path, an array of reasons will unveil themselves, similar to a cascading effect.

For me, the initial spark ignited at 43, facing my physical and emotional nadir. Weighing an awful 227 lbs., I encountered a stranger in the mirror. Simple tasks became herculean. Scoliosis, osteoarthritis, and plantar fasciitis among others intensified the struggle. Juggling family responsibilities, working in a pharmaceutical industry alongside caring for my ailing mother drained me every single day.

Appearances are not everything, but for certain people, they hold weight. It is not just physical; the emotional toll can be immense: depression, guilt, and anxiety wreaking chaos in our psyche. We scrutinize our past selves, reminiscing about our younger years. Even if our loved ones reassure us of our beauty, self-doubt creeps in, unraveling our confidence and self-esteem.

Each day, I questioned why I allowed myself to resemble someone I found 'ugly.' The embarrassment of feeling unrecognizable and unhealthy was profound. Physical discomfort turned mundane tasks into hurdles, eroding my self-worth.

Amidst the façade of laughter, an inner commotion brewed. Concealing my struggles, my days commenced with overwhelming responsibilities, a cycle of exhaustion and stress. No one truly grasped the turmoil within. Tears shed in solitude, the water washing away emotions, yet the unresolved feelings persisted—a relentless haunting. Deep down, I knew my beauty was still there. Ultimately, it is our souls and spirits that truly matter; our bodies are just vessels that hold them. But even with that knowledge, I still felt hideous.

Acknowledging my predicament was the initial step, embracing my own capabilities—the superpowers within. Why can I be a superhero for my kids, but not for myself? Admitting the need for help is where the transformation commences, setting off a chain reaction toward self-recovery.

These are all steps in a long healing process. It is Psychology 101... "Until the person admits they have a problem and needs help; they will not seek it out nor allow others to reach out to them." It is in that precise moment when the healing process begins, and like a domino effect, everything starts falling into place, like pieces of a puzzle.

Once we embrace our inner strengths, our superpowers, the potential for achievement knows no bounds. Trusting ourselves, irrespective of external opinions, becomes paramount for our upcoming quest.

CONSISTENCY, not perfection, marks our commitment to our 'end goals.' It is about evolving personally and professionally, being the best versions of ourselves, nurturing relationships, and self-love. This transformation odyssey is only possible remembering that you are committed to YOU, to your healing and self-love.

Altruism often stems from fulfilling personal desires and emotional needs. The journey commences with the aching to satisfy oneself, filling the emotional bucket. By helping ourselves, we become a light that guides others on their paths. We must trust and believe in our potential, regardless of what others may think.

ONE DAY OR DAY ONE.
"YOU DECIDE"

Embracing Challenges: The Essence of Life

Embracing life's challenges (wicked curves as I called those) is the heartbeat of a meaningful journey. If life were effortless, it would lack intrigue, rendering it monotonous. Periodically, we must venture beyond our comfort zones, shedding the protective cocoon, and willingly expose ourselves to vulnerabilities.

You might argue, "I fear vulnerability! What if my imperfections become fodder for others' ridicules? I am an expert in my domain, not a novice! I do not need assistance or

support!"

Well, newsflash... I have been there! I

have dared to be vulnerable. Over the past few

years, I have urged to share authentically, to

unveil my story—making it human with its highs

and lows—to resonate with others embarking

on their transformational journeys. Yet,

exposing myself on social media, revealing my

imperfections to an audience sometimes

unknown, was an entirely different challenge.

Since I started my transformation journey (in

2017 to be exact), while I posted as a coach

about my journey in fitness groups, revealing

struggles to relate with fellow challengers, the

plunge into social media's vulnerable space was

daunting. Acknowledging my personal

transformation—physically, mentally, and

emotionally—began amidst the uncertainty of

the Covid-19 era.

In 2020, amidst the pandemic's upheaval, I

found myself at a crossroads. My secure role in a

pharmaceutical firm faced closure, thrusting me

into uncertainty—a scenario people fear the

most, even me. It is not change but the

unpredictability and uncertainty that evoke fear,

despite professing beliefs like "Everything

happens for a Reason", "When a door closes, there are so many others opened. You have not seen those because you are focusing in the one "closing." and "Everything will be fine if you just Believe!"

The fear of uncertainty, especially an unpredictable future, is terrifying. Not knowing what lies ahead, what the next chapter of life will hold, or whether it will bring joy, and success can be deeply unsettling. This fear does not negate faith. It challenges the human psyche. Even when we advocate these beliefs, uncertainty can entangle us, and doubts creep in, playing mind games that leave us feeling desperate, hopeless, and sometimes even weak. In these moments, seeking help becomes crucial, building a support system of trusted allies. These are the fellow soldiers who will stand by you in your inner battles. They are the ones who will be there unconditionally, reminding you to harness your superpowers and to trust and believe in yourself.

personal transformation—physically, mentally, and emotionally—began amidst the uncertainty of the Covid-19 era.

In 2020, amidst the pandemic's upheaval, I found myself at a crossroads. My secure role in a pharmaceutical firm faced closure, thrusting me into uncertainty—a scenario people fear the most, even me. It is not change but the unpredictability and uncertainty that evoke fear, despite professing beliefs like "Everything happens for a Reason", "When a door closes, there are so many others opened. You have not seen those because you are focusing in the one "closing." and "Everything will be fine if you just Believe!"

Reflecting on my abilities and desires for the future, I contemplated what truly brought joy to my life and what talents I felt compelled to continue exploring. A once-abandoned list of passions resurfaced—set aside due to the

demands of my professional life. Despite

corporate's preaching about work-life balance, it

never quite felt that way for me (perhaps due to

my workaholic, highly responsible, goal-driven

nature). While I was taught that is not quantity,

yet quality of time what matters, the shift to

remote work during the 2020 Covid-19

pandemic unveiled the true joy of managing my

time and being able to spend more time with my

family – a precious time that whilst present, I

must admit it was not always to the fullest

potential

Living through a pandemic of epic proportions was no joke. It brought immense suffering to those who lost loved ones, and it sparked widespread desperation and anxiety. For others, it felt like being prisoners in their own homes. The pandemic truly transformed humankind as we once knew it. It was a pivoting moment in history. Changes became essential for the evolution and survival of our species, and we had to embrace those changes despite of the challenges – physically, emotionally, and mentally speaking.

During the pandemic, my pharmaceutical Regulatory Supervisor job role transitioned to a remote role which brought me newfound

flexibility, transforming holistically my routine. It

really gave me "flextime". I was able to wake up

later than usual since I did not have to drive 40-

minutes to commute. I was able to eat in my

home office (I was not allowed to do it in my

company office). I had meetings anywhere (even

walking a 10K in the neighborhood alongside my

husband).

This newfound perspective triggered a

chain reaction. With the pending closure of my

workplace, I delved into writing, a long-held

aspiration. I recall sitting at the dining table

writing late one night. I shared my work with my

daughters, and they encouraged me to compile

my scattered notes into a potential book (now a

reality).

Simultaneously, I rekindled my love for

arts and crafts. Encouraged by my daughters,

their words propelled me to consider creating an

online shop. Soon, with their support, I navigated

the realm of crafting and launched my shop

(www.Mimis-Shoppe.com).

Admitting imperfection and embracing

vulnerability catapulted me into uncharted

territories. The changes led to a shift in basic

assumptions (our own paradigms), allowing me

to manage time efficiently as a professional while

also exploring creative pursuits.

I must admit, this journey had not been

easy. Juggling a full-time professional job,

creating items for my shop every night after

finishing my professional duties, continuing

writing my book and ensuring I always made

time for myself, and my family was exhausting.

Grateful for the support of my family and my

trustworthy tribe (my support system), I

discovered a renewed purpose. Overcoming

reluctance, seeking empowerment, and

accepting uncertainty allowed me to embrace

what brings joy and peace.

Change can be frightening, yet it molds us into stronger beings—physically, mentally, and emotionally.   Seeking assistance is not a weakness; it is an emblem of courage. You might find yourself amid a challenging phase, feeling like it is the end. But trust me, it is not! It is your resilience, your human touch that propels success.

It is your willingness to move forward, keeping your life real – human, what will make you succeed. You are not alone on this journey. Dig deep within, find the courage to step beyond your comfort zone, and exceed your own expectations. Ready for a change? While I am not an expert, I have gathered tools and insights

that might aid you. It is all about shifting your

mindset.

WHO AM I?...
I AM
RESILIENT

Unveiling Resilience, Discovering Identity

Life's journey mirrors a rollercoaster ride. It cascades with peaks, troughs, and unforeseen twists that nudge us beyond our comfort zones. It is within these turbulent moments that our very essence is tested. Often, a single challenge can trigger a chain reaction, growing exponentially and leaving us feeling overwhelmed, emotionally drained, and occasionally questioning our own abilities – our superpowers. These are the times that help us build and strengthen our endurance

and resilience in life.

Resilience is not an overnight creation.

Resiliency is developed over time. Not

everyone swiftly rebounds from adversity,

pain, or sorrow. Yet, the capacity for resilience

is within us all. Life's challenges function as the

crucible for forging this resilience. While

selected people adapt faster, everyone can

develop this trait.

Often, resilience accompanies

adaptability and flexibility. It is about accepting

life's challenges, even the daunting ones. Is it

simple? No. But it is not unattainable. We must

embrace these changes, understanding that

they are essential for our growth and evolution.

We may not always welcome these changes,

but they are inevitable. We must grasp the

concepts: "Let go," "Detach," "This too shall

pass," "Learn from it," "Rise and persist," and

"Embrace adversity."

These concepts are the essential

building blocks for nurturing resilience—a

superpower akin to shapeshifting. Trust me, I

have been there. Life occasionally throws

merciless, painful moments our way. Those

times when we feel incapable of moving

forward. Moments that, despite our resistance, demand the utterance of "Let go" and "This too shall pass." While certain people remain fixated, others, in the process of cultivating resilience, take a different path.

I can recall my childhood years vividly, especially the times when I had taken a tumble and my father would say, "Ven acá pa' pararte". (Come over here so I can get you up). It is ironic how those words seemed almost magical. Instead of tears after a fall, I would put on a fiercely face and spring back up immediately, responding eagerly, "Ya me paré!" (I am already up!). It was as though those words of encouragement had a powerful effect,

instantly transforming my reaction to adversity.

Personally, the influence of parental

guidance and simple phrases like this one had

a profound impact, turning moments of

distress into displays of strength and

determination. It is a poignant illustration of

how positive words and encouragement can

shape a child's resilience in the face of

adversity. The support, coupled with

empowerment, that I received from an early

age has played a pivotal role in molding the

person I have become today.

Through deep reflection, I can honestly say that the harsh realities of life have also made me stronger: my parents' divorce on my 15th birthday, or the difficult experiences at school (what we now call bullying) simply because I was a nerd and the youngest in my class. No one, except my best friend at the time, knew about my family situation. It completely changed my outlook on life—how could it not? At fifteen, you believe your parents will always be together. Reality hit me hard, but I was too proud to let others see my sorrow. I wore a 'clown mask,' laughing on the outside while crying on the inside every day.

Despite everything, I channeled my energy into my studies, becoming top of my class and realizing my dream of starting college at 17 in the most prestigious Engineering college in Puerto Rico - University of Puerto Rico, Mayagüez Campus. I felt the urge to prove myself especially to my parents (most of all, my dad). I strongly believe it was an emotional rebellion for "leaving us". It was my way to tell him once again, "I do not need your help. I am standing on my own and will keep getting back up after every fall. I am unstoppable."

The crux lies in stepping back and observing the situation from a different angle—a fresh perspective, a new mindset. It is

no easy feat; emotions cloud our judgment,

obscuring rationality. In these crucial moments,

remember, you are not alone.

Occasionally, life demands vulnerability—

opening to others, seeking aid. Establishing a

support system is vital. Whether a partner,

family member, or trusted friend, they offer

diverse perspectives. Regardless of the

sometimes-brutal truths, their insights aid in

finding solutions, fostering physical, emotional,

and mental well-being, granting the inner peace

you deserve.

Imagine this process as a boxer in the ring, exchanging punches, falling, then rising amidst the crowd's rallying cries; "Come on, get up! Do not give up! You got this!". Every fall comes with encouragement to stand, fight, and persist—with greater agility and strength.

That is the spirit! That is resilience. You might argue, "Even if the boxer wins or loses, there is a lot of money involved." True, money can be a substantial motivator. But what is your driver? Mine is my family. They are the reason I wake up every morning to deal with my responsibilities (whether I like it or not.) Discovering your motivation is what propels you beyond challenges. And yes, you can—I

guarantee it. It will take time, rewiring your

brain. It is not merely the pursuit of happiness

(after all happiness is just an emotional state

that shifts and changes in a blink of an eye). It is

the pursuit of purpose—your "Lo scopo della

vita" (your life's purpose). Discovering your

purpose makes life meaningful, filling your heart

with fervor. It is finding your center ensuring

you fill-up your emotional bucket. Your true

purpose might not align with daily

responsibilities or your profession. Take my

case for example: a Mechanical Engineering with

a minor in Psychology graduate with a passion

for writing and entrepreneurship—entirely

unrelated to my studies. Believe me, I enjoyed

truly my studies and career. Yet, the curse of life

transformed my odyssey with each decision I

faced and the choices I made along the way.

Remember, you are not alone. Your

support system offers a non-judgmental

sanctuary. This transition becomes more

manageable with their presence. Struggling

through tough times does not signify failure; it

signifies growing resilience and adaptability.

Regardless of life's "wicked curves",

consider those a lesson; an opportunity—a step

closer to your best self, ready to excel and face

future challenges with unwavering confidence.

Learn to trust and embrace yourself and your

inner wisdom. You are capable of making

S-M-A-R-T decisions. Stay focused and plan for

the opportunities that will benefit your future.

This is the time to walk away from things and

people that disappoint you (even toxic family

members if you ask me). You must not feel

guilting for "letting go". This is being wiser not

ruthless. This is "self-love". It is about prioritizing

your emotional well-being. You do not need to

stay attached to people or situations that weigh

you down. Your support system should be those

that will always lift you up and will remind you

to stay standing tall. Do not let the

opportunities slip through your fingers by

staying focused on the past and the wrong

relationships. Holding on to what no longer

serves you can prevent you from moving

forward. Keep your eyes on the future and the

connections that truly matter; those that

support your wellbeing.

Remember:
"You are in the Driver's seat."

Chapter 4   # Steering YOUR Life

"Having a clear objective is crucial for achieving flow;
however, we must also learn to leave it behind
when we get down to business." –García and Miralles

Having a goal in sight keeps us on the

path toward that "End Zone," our desired

destination. Yet, fixating on the goal can breed

anxiety, leading to a negative impact. When

progress toward the "end zone" is not as swift

as anticipated, it often leads to frustration and

self-doubt. Despite previous efforts, we might

even contemplate quitting, failing ourselves all

over again.

Time alone is not the solution to reaching the "end zone." The crucial element is consistency. Hurdles and milestones will always punctuate our journey—after all, that is life! Our determination and ardent desire to achieve successful outcomes, to feel accomplished upon reaching the objective, fuel our journey. It is the passion invested that gives us a sense of fulfillment at the "end" of the journey, energizing us and sparking a renewed desire to accomplish more, prolonging our lives.

Arriving at the "end zone" does not signal the end; it merely denotes the completion of a specific goal, priming us for a new objective, a new project, a new "end zone."

However, this time, it is different. It

feels different. Filled with energy and

enthusiasm from the previous achievement, we

approach this new endeavor with an altered

perspective, a transformed mindset.

Now, we are certain that we can achieve

anything we set our minds to. I mean, why not?

We have just done it. Life offers choices, but

understanding HOW to live our lives depends on

how well we comprehend our WHY.

How do you recognize YOUR WHY? It is

simple. Ask yourself: What fills your emotional

bucket? What motivates you every single day?

What stirs your passion? In other words, what is

the reason you wake up every day, ready to face

challenges and accomplish something

meaningful, feeling content and at peace? For

me, it is my family. Those who know me can

affirm that I always say: "My family is my Driver!"

They are my reason for waking up daily, driven

to work and provide, both professionally and

personally. Yes, I have a career I enjoy, but it is

my family's support in all aspects that propels

me forward. That is my WHY. Their support

drives me to care for myself because I have

learned the hard way that neglecting self-care

impedes my ability to care for them.

Self-care is not selfish; it is essential for

physical, mental, and emotional well-being. It is

an act of love that maintains our sanity and

restores lost energy, allowing us to pursue our

"end-goals." Amidst these goals, we must

remind ourselves not to obsess but to drive our

lives at a steady pace—not too fast, never too

slow.

Visual reminders of our WHYs in specific

places help maintain focus. For me, it is the

refrigerator door, my office, home gym, even

my bedside table. Undoubtedly, you have your

"special" places too—those areas serving as

reminders of your WHY and HOW to achieve

your "end goal."

As authors García and Miralles suggest in

their book "Ikigai" (a highly recommended

read): "Concentrating on one thing at a time

may be the single most important factor in

achieving flow." Flow signifies a moment in life

when we are immersed in an experience, free

from distractions. Is it easy to achieve? To be

completely transparent, on a personal level,

discovering what truly resonates with me has

taken years. I have developed a love for various

hobbies and learned that depending on my

emotional state, I utilize certain hobbies to de-

stress and rejuvenate.

Surprisingly, it is during emotional

times—when I am sad or angry—that I often

perform at my best. When angry, my workouts

become my best, fueled by extra adrenaline that

makes me faster and stronger. Eventually,

releasing those endorphins during the workout

helps restore a better state of mind. When I am

cheerful, I allow myself to explore new things,

new creations letting my imagination run wild.

Sadness, on the other hand, often leads to my

best creative outputs, whether in drawing,

painting, or writing. That paper or canvas becomes my outlet to express my deepest emotions—a judgment-free zone!

To find that "flow," rushing is never the answer. Let emotions run wild and savor every moment as if it were the last. Live your DREAM life. Sometimes, we get caught up in excuses like "I need to save for retirement" or "I don't have time for _____ (fill in YOUR blank)." Yes, saving for retirement and managing time are vital, but finding moments and routines that emotionally fulfill us is equally crucial. We do not need to be sad or angry to create masterpieces—we ARE masterpieces!

Unfortunately, we often overlook our own grace, merely passing through life. It is only when someone else notices certain traits or changes in us that we reflect on our accomplishments, particularly those achieved during our struggles—the ones we should cherish most, as they have offered us the most growth.

The challenge of "flow" is not in discovering it yet in maintaining it. In this modern world, achieving undistracted focus—a prerequisite for full immersion in any task—is itself a daunting task. We are inseparable from our cell phones, constantly bombarded with messages, emails, and the allure of social media platforms. Finding that "ME" time to connect with our inner selves,

discovering and maintaining the flow, is a

constant struggle. Distractions are not limited to

technology; they can stem from work, family, or

friends—anything that disrupts the flow. Whilst

these distractions may sometimes be necessary,

we must rethink how to sustain flow. We need

to reinvent ourselves, altering or modifying

habits. This is how we will master the art of

change.

For instance, waking up a little earlier to enjoy

distraction-free solitude before the family rises

can provide that much-needed personal time.

This extra time grants the opportunity for

gratitude practice, prayer, reading and

journaling while sipping your morning coffee or

tea, a quick workout or meditation practice.

Performing one or a combination is a perfect

way to start the day. Conversely, for those who

prefer extra sleep, an evening routine might be

beneficial. Try doing a quick workout or

meditation to have a stress relief activity from

your busy day. Take a well-deserved and

relaxing bath using some aromatherapy and

relaxing music, eat healthy and read a book plus

journaling about what you read or about your

day, and detox from technology if you can. You

can use aromatherapy with candles, incense, music; those can help set the tone to relax and have a better sleep. Plus, do not forget to prepare for the next day. I have found that having an evening routine sets the tone to have a more successful morning start. Whichever your routine, just make it your own... and remember you can change it and/or modify it whenever you need to. It is all about YOU! It is all about what helps you find flow and maintain it.

My advice: focus on one task at a time. Yes, I understand—you have multiple projects to complete. I can completely relate. In today's work culture, companies often seek

'multitaskers,' which sounds great for them but

can be exhausting for the individual. Time

management courses have taught me valuable

techniques for distinguishing between urgent

tasks, priorities, and those wishful to-dos. While

everything needs to be done, I have found that

creating a list of tasks helps me concentrate on

one at a time. Checking off completed tasks

fuels the momentum to keep going with the

remaining ones. I use this technique not only at

work, but also in my personal life.

Self-Care = Self Love

Chapter 5   Nourishing Your Spirit

Sleep and rest are vital for the body to recover and come back stronger to our daily routines. In my journey, I have seen my sleeping habits transform since 1991. I remember my childhood days when my mom used to say, "There could be a world catastrophe, and you would not even notice!" Ah, those were the days! I could sleep for long hours, and nothing could disturb my slumber. Oh, how I miss those moments!

However, everything changed in the blink of an eye when I became a mother for the first time. I believe all moms can relate. I started waking up even before my babies stirred from their naps. I could sense their cries before they even began. It is that maternal intuition or sixth sense that altered my sleep patterns forever. Trying to understand this shift, I have different clues. As adults, our plates overflow with worries—family, kids, finances, jobs, household duties, saving for college, planning vacations, and trying to secure a stable future. The list goes on and on, doesn't it?

Recognizing that sleep, rest, and attuning to my body are crucial for quicker healing has become essential for me. Sometimes, it is not only physical healing from an injury, an intense workout, or a DIY project. Often, it is about emotional healing, allowing the mind and soul to take a break from incessant worries.

Occasionally, taking a mental hiatus from a nagging issue can work wonders. Detoxing emotionally helps us regain the energy necessary to confront problems like champions. It rejuvenates us, refocuses our thoughts, allowing us to explore diverse solutions. Not every swing will hit a homerun at first; it takes practice. Just like in sports or the arts, practice differentiates mediocrity from greatness or excellence. Answers will not always be readily available for every challenge life throws at us, and that is precisely why we cannot afford to rest.

Let us be real! Several of us cannot sit still for extended periods. Even when our bodies beg for a break, our minds persistently urge us to keep moving, striving to complete the next task for a sense of accomplishment. We crave that golden solution to fix whatever problem we are tackling, whether personal or professional. We dig deeper into ourselves to analyze what is amiss, especially during our transformational journey.

I can tell you that being a caregiver for more than half of my life pushed me into a corner and knocked me down. Caregivers often prioritize everyone else, relegating self-care to the bottom of an extensive list. Exhaustion becomes a constant companion. We push ourselves harder each day forgetting how crucial it is to love and care for ourselves first. I have felt guilty too, but I have learned that those 15 to 30 minutes I take for myself each day, that "ALONE ME TIME," is the most effective emotional detox I could ask for.

As caregivers, we often learn (usually the hard way) that we must make ourselves the #1 priority, and that is not being selfish. In fact, it is an act of greater love not only for us, but also those we care for. The best version of ourselves brings out the best among those around us as well. Yet, it is always a struggle. The caregiver in you will always say, 'You need to take care of them,' while your inner voice is quietly reminding you, 'You need to take care of yourself. If you do not, who will be there to care for them?'

You need to reset and find time for yourself—time to do what truly pleases you and lifts your spirit. Only then you can recharge and continue caring for those you love, whether it is your spouse, kids, or like in my case, your ill parents.

It does not matter how or where you recharge. It could be in the comfort of your home, watching a great movie or show, cooking a delicious meal (a feast if you will), going to the gym, taking a walk in the park, volunteering for a cause dear to your heart, or even just sleeping. What matters is that you listen to your body and take time when you need it.

Most of the time, we believe we are strong, independent, unstoppable, capable of achieving anything we set our minds to. But even superheroes need time to recharge and regain the strength to keep fighting. You too are a fierce warrior, but as human beings, we all need those moments to re-energize, recharge and find our inner strength again.

Going back to "Memory Lane" and reflecting on those final days of my mother's illness, when Alzheimer's and other conditions had taken so much from her, there were still moments of clarity where she would urge me to take care of myself. She would say, "Princesa, prométeme que te vas a cuidar para que sigas cuidando de tu familia" (Princess, promise me you will take care of yourself so you can continue caring for your family). After she passed and became my guardian angel, her words stayed with me, especially in moments when I felt no desire, moments of hopelessness or depression. They gave me the strength to keep fighting for what I believe in and to defend my family—my reason to keep pushing forward and shining every day. Her wisdom reminds me to lead by example, to "walk the talk."

Methods for Emotional detox vary for each person. What works for me might not work for you. Our personalities and coping mechanisms differ because we each possess unique superpowers. I have different methods I use to manage my emotional rollercoaster. There are days that I jot down thoughts on a piece of paper—a non-judgmental space to unload my mind. Other times, I let my creativity flow through drawing. I love cooking; therefore, sometimes I indulge in preparing a feast, expressing myself through culinary creations. Then there are days when I go for a run with my intense Latin music, letting my mind roam free and go wild. And sometimes, I hit the home gym and tackle the boxing bag as if I were a UFC pro—better than Ronda Rousey, even! These activities let me physically vent what is troubling my mind. Moreover,

these methods allow my endorphins to surface

again, restoring my inner peace and balance.

Finding your center, your equilibrium,

and a coping mechanism that resonates with

you is crucial. Our emotions can divert us from

our purpose if left unchecked. It is not always an

easy task to grapple with emotions and give our

soul the rest it needs. We must search for that

"Leap of Faith," that "light at the end of the

tunnel" to reach our "Paradise City," right?

Taking that leap on the emotional rollercoaster

and reaching the end zone is essential. Life will

always have difficulties (those rollercoaster's ups

and downs). I always say, "It is not about how many times we fall, but how many times we get up and remain standing after that fall!"

Understanding that our emotional turbulence exceeds the speed of sound by fivefold marks the initial stride toward our triumph. This realization holds immense power in our lives. At times, we must acknowledge that we are not solitary entities and that concealing our emotions within a protective shell is not always feasible. Yes, vulnerability can be daunting, yet it affords others a genuine glimpse into our authentic selves. Moreover, it assures them they are not alone on their own journeys. Embracing vulnerability may seem intimidating, yet it allows

others to recognize that whilst we differ, we all

grapple with challenges, milestones, and sacrifices

that collectively propel us toward becoming

improved versions of ourselves.

Discovering a coping mechanism and

support system that suits you is crucial.

Emotional detox rejuvenates the spirit, granting

the soul the rest it deserves. Remember, do not

overwhelm yourself by trying to fix everything at

once. Knock down one thing at a time. The

sense of accomplishment will propel you to

tackle the next challenge on your list.

In the midst of your self-discovery, as you unwind deeper into your past to continue your transformation, you may find regrets creeping in, trying to disrupt your progress. Give yourself grace and accept who you are, even that 'Darth Vader' side of you. You might feel disappointed, disengaged, dissatisfied, and unmotivated. These are red flags. This is the moment to re-evaluate and reconnect with the greater purpose in your life. Be strategic on how you approach this process. This process can often be harsh. Deep wounds must be addressed once and for all and only you have the power to free yourself from those painful moments, regrets, and people.

Express your inner thoughts instead of bottling them up. You might feel torn between seeking help or keeping everything to yourself—I have been there. Pride often tells us we must survive on our own, to be self-sufficient. However, it is in the darkest times that you find yourself doing what is right for you and those you love, even if it means swallowing that pride. My parents used to say, 'It is in the tough times that you truly see who cares for you.' And trust me, those are wise words.

Remember, you are not a quitter, you are a finisher! Give yourself some grace, allow time to heal and be grateful for every moment and every person who helps you move one step

forward in your journey. Forgive yourself and

those who have hurt you. Yes, I know it is not

easy. But think about it for a brief moment-

holding on to that bitterness only restrains you.

The other person (even your past self) will never

feel the pain you are carrying, especially if you

do not express it.

And just to be clear, I am saying forgive

not forget. You will not genuinely forget what

happened in the past. But with time and if you

try hard enough you can tuck it away it into that

side of the mind that "boxes up" those not so

good or irrelevant remembrances. That does not

mean that it will not resurface if something

triggers it. It also does not mean it has to

control your present. You are transforming your

life, and you are the captain of your ship. You

are rebuilding yourself to the ground up with a

better foundation, a stable one so strong that

will help you navigate into the most turbulent

waters moving forward. This time, you can look

into the future with a positive mindset.

Remember that wisdom is the present that

comes from past experiences.

Chapter 6

The Influence of Energy: Choosing Wisely

There are people that refer to it as

Energy, Vibes, or Karma—good or evil. However,

labeled, this is one aspect where the laws of

science—where positive and negative

attractions do not hold true. What remains

factual is that the energy encompassing you

significantly impacts not just your life; but also,

those around you. When you resonate with

positivity, radiating good vibes and performing

benevolent acts, positivity naturally gravitates

towards you. Why? Because these positive

energies, vibes, or karma empower you to face each day with vigor, live joyfully, and become not simply better for yourself, yet for everyone you love, extending to even those unknown to you, nurturing a drive to enrich their lives.

Starting each day with gratitude, acknowledging both the outstanding and the less-than-ideal experiences (since they teach us valuable lessons), is a choice to evolve into a superior version of oneself. Each righteous decision made tramples the beast—bad karma, negative energy—and ensures it does not cause harm to you or your loved ones. It ensures your physical, emotional, and mental well-being.

Ever heard of "Pay it forward"? It is a true adage. Say you needed help, and someone lent you a hand. The gratitude you feel sparks a desire to help others experience that same feeling. Consequently, the person you assist, then feels gratitude and, in turn, extends their help. This forms a powerful nuclear chain reaction, motivating and inspiring others to improve themselves. Moreover, your impactful deeds do not just affect the individual you helped, yet also others around, even those observing from a distance. They will be inclined to follow suit, akin to the "Monkey see, monkey do" concept. Your positive actions, observed by others, generate an even larger ripple effect

than anticipated.

However, when you permit negative

vibes to infiltrate your life, you set yourself on a

downward path. It leads to increased anger,

depression, frustration, draining your energy to

move forward. You will not only be impacting

your life; but also, the one of your family and

everyone in your circle. Be honest with yourself,

courageous enough to recognize when you

need help and ask for it. Asking for help is not a

sign of weakness; it signifies bravery and

courage.

What you might overlook is that when dark emotions cloud your judgment, they also affect others. Picture this: your brain switches to survival mode, focusing on safety. Consider a crying baby—initially, we rush to address their needs. But when the baby seeks attention over and over, we become indifferent, unresponsive, and apathetic. We think that it is time for them to learn to self-sooth. This pattern, when consistently exhibited, may lead to a similar response from those around us.

Just as we become indifferent to the crying baby, others might adopt a protective mechanism towards us, avoiding negativity. Life is not always smooth sailing, but persistent bad vibes every day are draining. It is within our power to delve into our emotions and make the right choices. Summon the courage to be your own superhero.

Now that you are aware, the choice has always been yours. Will you embrace Good Energy, Vibes, Karma to uplift your life, propel you forward, and bring out the best in you? Or will you allow Bad Energy, Bad Vibes, Bad Karma to engulf you, making you and those around you miserable? What is your choice?

Chapter 7

Voyage

"The real voyage of discovery consists not in seeking new landscapes, but in having new eyes." – Marcel Proust

There are times in life when we, as humans, find ourselves uncertain about our own struggles. We might be adrift, unsure of where to navigate next. I do not know about you, but I have definitely been there many times in my life. Life is a cycle—sometimes things repeat, whether for good or to ensure we learn the lessons we need to so we can move forward.

I know I am not the only one on this voyage. Often, we wander around searching for new "places", forgetting that our first step should be to dig deeper within ourselves. We need to analyze what has happened and determine what comes next. Taking our circumstances into account, it is important to reflect on what has changed—if anything. Sometimes, the world around us remains the same, but inside, we have shifted. We may have grown, learned the lessons we were meant to, or matured beyond a former version of ourselves. Perhaps we have reached a milestone, opening our hearts, minds, and spirits to new beginnings—a new voyage. Over time, we adapt, growing stronger through the lessons that life teaches us.

I have learned to call those lessons "opportunities in life". Too often, people mistakenly believe they have failed when things do not turn out as expected. But my wise mother used to say: "Todo depende del cristal con el que se miran las cosas" which translate to: "It all depends on the lens through which you view things". She always encouraged us to chase our dreams, never stop, and keep fighting for what we believed in and for what was right.

I learned early on—ever since I was a teenager—that in order to achieve anything in life, to realize any of those dreams, I had to know myself first. Understanding both my strengths and weaknesses would be crucial to my own journey, and to the journeys of those whose lives I would 'touch' in one way or another.

You must first understand yourself in order to utterly understand others. For some people, this is an incredibly challenging task. Many assume they know themselves, but do we all truly and deeply know who we are? Sometimes, it is the little or simple things that reveal who we are—like knowing your favorite food, colors, or what triggers your emotions. That, my friend, is the voyage of self-discovery. It is not an easy journey, especially when it comes to recognizing your "weaker side". No one likes to feel weak, and most of us do not want to depend on others all the time (I know I certainly do not). Even at 51, I still struggle with asking for help.

I was raised to be a strong, independent woman, but I can confess there have been times when I have felt utterly hopeless, knocked down by the wicked curves life threw my way. I am deeply grateful to my family and my 'Cara

Amica' for always being there during those moments when I felt lost. Having them as my support system has been a constant reminder that I am not alone on my journey.

It is a reminder that, even though life can be uncertain, and despite being a strong woman, I can rely on them. I can be vulnerable and feel at ease with them because I know that no matter what, they have my back. They provide a judgment-free zone where I can express myself freely. They help me recalibrate and redirect my navigation guiding me when I lose my way, like my own personal North Star.

Not everyone's journey is the same.

Losing loved ones is devastating, and while some people may be enjoying life with their families, there are those, like me, who have lost the people dearest to them—my parents, Sotero and Esther; my baby, Bryan Joshua; and my grandparents, Ernesto and Iris. I know they are with us in spirit, watching over us as our angels, but holidays and special moments are no longer the same. We remember them by reminiscing, talking about how things were when they were alive. Now, we cherish the memories—how we cooked together, played dominoes, danced, and laughed.

People these days often forget to be empathetic. Yes, you can enjoy life; but also, consider those who feel depressed or alone, even in a room full of people. Everyone's experience is different.

Life changes us every second. It does not waste time. So why do we stubbornly hold on to the past? Why do we keep asking, "What if?" Why do we doubt ourselves or hesitate when faced with decisions that could change our future? Simple—we are afraid. Afraid to take that leap of faith. Afraid of failing if things do not go as planned. But sometimes we must make those tough decisions and have hope. We need to understand that we can achieve

anything we set our minds to. Will it be easy?

No, of course not. But that is what makes life's

journey challenging, interesting, and rewarding.

There are no failures—only challenges and

milestones to overcome.

I was raised in a family that taught me to

fight for my dreams and pursue the life I want.

Growing up with this mindset shaped me into

someone who is both realistic and optimistic. It

made me realize that I do not just want to chase

a dream life; I want to live it. And to do that, I

need to change, adapt, and be incredibly

resilient. It will not always go the way I want

right away, and solutions do not always appear

instantly. But when your mind and heart are

aligned and focused on success, it will come—in

its own time. And when it does, you will be able

to check that milestone off your list and move

on to the next one.

I do not believe in a "final destination". Every destination is just the beginning of a new one. Once you reach one goal, you are already thinking about the next. This time, it is a little easier, because reaching that previous goal has equipped you with new tools—courage, heart, and a positive 'can-do' mindset. The next challenge may still be uncertain, but you are not as afraid as you were before. You made it once,

and that means you can keep doing it

repeatedly, until you decide to stop.

Remember, you are the captain of your

journey. No matter which routes you take, as

long as you stay true to yourself, you are not

afraid to ask for help when you need it, and take

that leap of faith in yourself, you will reach the

next destination. Every step brings you closer to

living your dream life. Do not waste time

doubting yourself—go for it! No one else is

going to do it for you. If you want something in

life, you must do the work. So, what are you

waiting for? The only thing standing between

you and your next destination is you!

BLOOM WHERE
YOU ARE PLANTED

Blooming in Life

Like the flower that blooms and attracts

the bees, you cannot assume that all the things

you desire in life will come to you effortlessly.

We are not in the wizarding world that you will

say: "Alohomora" and the doors will magically

open. Sure, that would be amazing (do not get

me wrong); but it would not be rewarding.

If everything you desire comes to you in

the blink of an eye like wishes granted by a

"genie in a bottle" the real you will never

blossom. Instead of mastering life, you would become its puppet. You might feel temporary happiness when you get what you want immediately, but as I always say, "Happiness is a fleeting emotional state." One moment you are happy, and in the next, that feeling can transform into sadness or anger.

There is no greater feeling than the satisfaction of completing something and being able to say, 'I did it!' No one can take away that sense of accomplishment, the credit for the tears, laughter, frustration, and those 'Aha!' moments that lead you to bloom. Those are *your* moments, and they are yours to keep. What is even better is that when you fill your emotional

bucket with that sense of achievement, you are

ready to blossom again. And this time, it is

easier—or at least less stressful—because you

have done it before. You are no longer starting

from scratch. You can now tweak, adjust, and

make it even better. This is what I call life's

"continuous improvement process 101".

We all need to adapt and evolve with

change. Sure, staying in a comfort zone sounds

appealing, but ask yourself—do you really grow

by staying static? I do not know about you, but

while I am a great swimmer, I do not want to

stay in the "comfort zone" of a sinking boat. I

want to be sailing on a vast, majestic cruise, navigating life's endless opportunities.

Just like flowers need daily watering and fertile soil to bloom, you need to nurture yourself in life. Keep learning, keep growing. Make yourself 'marketable' for new opportunities. Always seek ways to improve and continue to shine. When you do, you are not only progressing on your own journey, but you are also showing others that they can do it too. You are setting an example for continuous growth.

Unbelievably, someone is always watching all your moves even from a distance.

For example... I recalled when I was working out

after coming home from work (not only to lose

those extra pounds but also to de-stress). I

would arrange my mat, my weights, drink my

energize and prepare my hydrate. I then set my

favorite workout Trainers' program (LIIFT4 or 10

Rounds from Joel Freeman) or (Insanity, T-25, or

Transform 20 from Shaun T). All of a sudden, I

saw how my daughter joined me and from a

distance, my grandbaby would join too. She

was in Pre-K at the time (you do the math). She

would grab a towel (instead of a mat), a bottle

of water (instead of the hydrate) and the 2-lbs

and 3-lbs weights (instead of the heavy 10-lbs

to 20-lbs her mom and I used). She would

follow the instructions of the trainers to the "T".

After seeing this for a couple of days, it became

our family routine. We ended up buying her,

her own mat. Without even thinking about it, I

was leading by example.

Once the workout session concluded, we

would take a picture together. I would post the

picture with a motivational message in my

Beachbody coaching team. Let us face it,

having a 4–5-year-old kid doing those fitness

exercises, can be an emotional challenge to

some people. Hopefully, it would ignite their

inner child and their competitive mentality of "if

she can, I certainly can do it too." I know it did

ignite mine for sure. I wanted to ensure I was

able to run and have fun with her for the

longest time in my life. I am a young grandma

("Abu" as she calls me) after all. I did not want

to miss any of that just because of the everyday

excuses... "I am tired from all day at work.", "I

am in pain (with all my illnesses)" and any other

excuse I could find (as we all do).

This is your time to think of those "even at a

distance" moments in your life. We all have

those. You might need to go into "Memory

Lane" and corner "Trust Your Heart". Place your

efforts in remembering all those things you do

in life, in your day-to-day activities. This is a

time to reflect on what you do, how you do it

and what you can do differently to make a

positive impact not only for you yet also to all

those around you. Jog down your memories,

find the gratifying moments and those that are

opportunities to take a different path... to

ensure you are ready to blossom no matter

where you are planted.

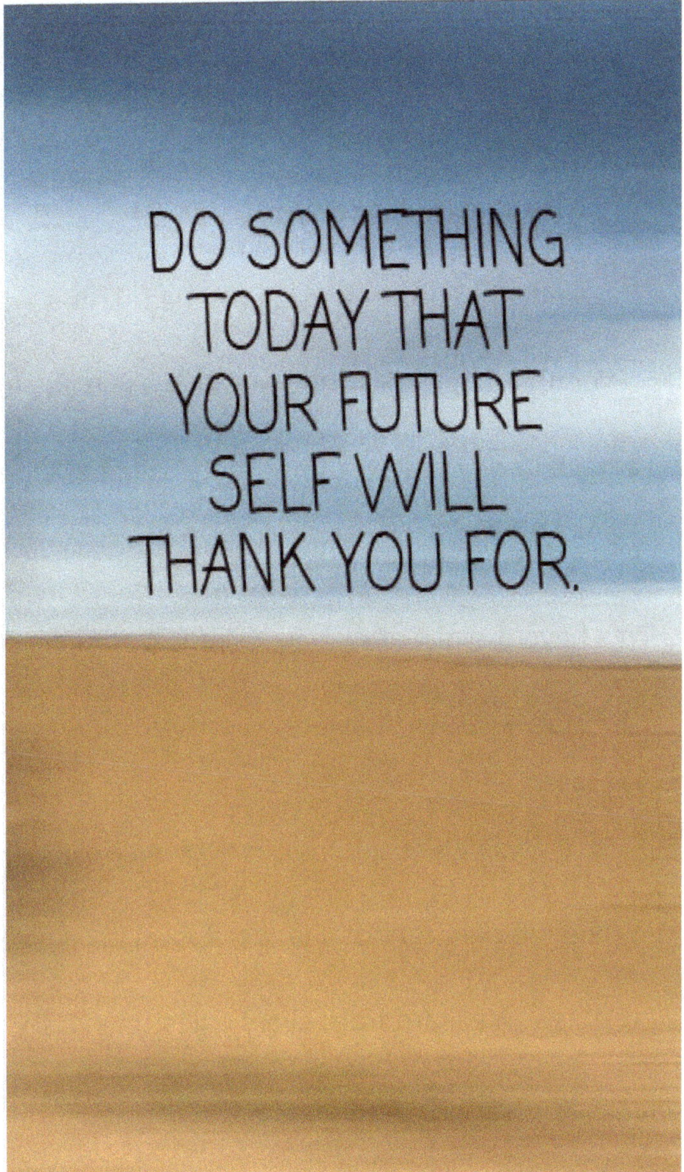

DO SOMETHING
TODAY THAT
YOUR FUTURE
SELF WILL
THANK YOU FOR.

Every Choice Shapes Your Now

If you know me, you have heard me say: "Everything in life is foreseen!" and "Each day is a fresh beginning, an opportunity to gain experience, learn, and become our best selves." We have the gift of human will, the power of decision—yes, the Power of Decision!

This power shapes our lives every day. While the past cannot change, it is an invaluable teacher. We learn from every milestone, both the extraordinary and the defining moments

that leave a scar in our lives.

Our choices have been the driver,

guiding us to this very moment. We have the

power to decide, to chart our fate. While some

things remain beyond our control, for those

within our grasp, we can prioritize what truly

matters, caring for ourselves and others.

Cultivating a chain reaction of positivity can

inspire a better world for all.

Contemplate your aspirations, your

purpose in life, and work towards it. Each step

inches you closer to transforming your dream

life into reality. Every choice you have made has brought you to this moment. Now, the path your life takes hinges entirely on the decisions you make ahead. Use your superpower of Decision wisely!

Embrace life's challenges; they are essential for growth. Prepare for uncertainties by planning for the future. Life will throw unexpected, wicked curveballs, but planning equips you to be flexible, adaptable. If you are uncertain, seek guidance. Be open to adopting proven ideas; there is no shame in not reinventing the wheel ("steal with pride"). If a strategy does not work for you, adapt it, and

modify it so you can develop your own.

Remember, it is okay to fail. Fear the

regret for not trying more than failing itself. If

you stumble, rise like a boxer, stronger and

braver than before. Think of every fall as an

opportunity to raise stronger and wiser. Do not

let anyone interfere with your future best

version of yourself. Use these falls as a moment

to redirect your path, to learn and progress.

As Laozi once said, "The journey of a

thousand miles begins with a single step."

Think back to your infant self-learning to walk.

You crawled, grabbed onto support, stood, balanced, and took your first steps. We all go through a similar process. At times, dive into your deepest emotions, even when the truths are harsh. Progress in life demands honesty with oneself.

Consider the traits inherited from your parents—learn from them, striving to become better versions, more adaptable to the times we live in. Unearth your inner strengths, identifying the superpowers that will help you achieve what seems to be the 'impossible.' These abilities pave the way for a meaningful life with purpose.

Remember, you are not alone on this transformative journey! Asking for help is not a sign of weakness but of courage and bravery. Build your support system. Believe me, we all need one. They help us be accountable of our actions, hear our thoughts and if you choose wisely, they will be available for you at any time to hear without judgement your emotions. You should be able to trust your support system.

Often, people tend to work in silos (guilty as charge). Sometimes it is needed; do not get me wrong. We need to explore ideas of our own; however, collaboration often surpasses solitary efforts. Working together, understanding diverse ideas, strengthens us collectively. Listening to others to ensure that we can make a united difference. Every once in a blue moon, we are not going to agree with others, but if we listen instead of hearing, we will understand that there is always a reason behind their actions, ideas, or feelings. My wise mother used to say "ponte en los zapatos de los demás" (put yourself in the other person's shoes). Meaning, try to understand their thoughts and feelings – their perspective.

Nurture your mind, body, and emotions in balance. This harmony fosters resilience and purpose. Grant yourself moments of relaxation amidst adversity, learning to cope and emerge

stronger. Disconnect to reconnect—with loved

ones, nature, and, most importantly, with

yourself. Self-discovery paves the way for a

robust return.

Now is your time to change, to adapt,

and to be flexible. It is time to learn from the

opportunities' life presents and continue

shaping an updated version of yourself.

Remember, you are not competing with anyone

else. You are only striving to be better than

who you were yesterday. There is no greater

way to show self-care and self-love than by

showing up for yourself every single day. There

will be days that you will hesitate – days that

might slow you down, but it is up to you if you

decide to stop.

Our actions and decisions today will

shape the way we will be living in the future.

Are you ready to begin your transformation

odyssey? Are you ready to excel in life? What

are you waiting to start your self-discovery and

set sail into your transformation odyssey? No

one can stop you if you believe in your own

superpowers.

www.ingramcontent.com/pod-product-compliance
Lightning Source LLC
Chambersburg PA
CBHW050541160726

48003CB00002B/692